Para mama, Serve, Luna y Pablo, y por supuesto Holita — me llenan el corazón de arroz con leche. — **JA**

Para mi dulce compañera, Stela. — **FV**

For my mother, Serve, Luna and Pablo, and of course Holita — they fill my heart with rice pudding. — **JA**

To my sweet wife, Stela. — **FV**

————

NOTA

Todas las etapas de la receta que vienen marcadas con * requieren la participación o supervisión de un adulto.

NOTE

All stages of the recipe that are marked * require the participation or supervision of an adult.

————

Text copyright © 2010 by Jorge Argueta
Illustrations copyright © 2010 by Fernando Vilela
Published in Canada and the USA in 2010 by Groundwood Books
First paperback edition 2016
Third printing 2021

Groundwood Books / House of Anansi Press
groundwoodbooks.com

Groundwood Books respectfully acknowledges that the land on which we operate is the traditional territory of many nations, including the Mississaugas of the Credit, the Anishnabeg, the Chippewa, the Haudenosaunee and the Wendat peoples.

We gratefully acknowledge for its financial support of our publishing program the Government of Canada.

With the participation of the Government of Canada
Avec la participation du gouvernement du Canada | Canadä

Library and Archives Canada Cataloguing in Publication
Argueta, Jorge, author
Arroz con leche : un poema para cocinar = Rice pudding : a cooking poem / written by Jorge Argueta ; illustrated by Fernando Vilela.
Previously published by Groundwood Books, 2010.
Text in Spanish and English.
ISBN 978-1-55498-887-7 (pbk)
1. Rice puddings—Juvenile poetry. 2. Cooking—Juvenile poetry.
3. Children's poetry, Salvadoran. I. Vilela, Fernando, illustrator
II. Title. III. Title: Rice pudding.
PQ7539.2.A67A77 2016   j861'.64   C2015-904634-3

Design by Michael Solomon
Printed and bound in Malaysia

ARROZ CON LECHE

RICE PUDDING

Un poema para cocinar

·

A Cooking Poem

ESCRITO POR / WORDS BY

JORGE ARGUETA

ILUSTRADO POR / PICTURES BY

FERNANDO VILELA

GROUNDWOOD BOOKS
HOUSE OF ANANSI PRESS
TORONTO BERKELEY

Me gusta el arroz de todas las formas.
Me gusta el arroz blanco
el arroz moreno
el arroz frito
el arroz sancochado
el arroz aguado
el arroz con frijoles
el arroz con pollo.
En fin, me encanta el arroz con todo.
Pero lo que más me gusta y me fascina
es el arroz con leche.

I like all kinds of rice.
I like white rice,
brown rice,
fried rice,
stewed rice,
watery rice,
chicken and rice,
beans and rice.
I guess I like rice with anything.
But what I like best and love the most
is rice pudding.

El arroz con leche
se hace así.
Uno necesita
una olla.

You make rice pudding
like this.
First you need
a pot.

Y necesitas dos tazas de arroz
dos tazas de agua
unas rajitas de canela
cuatro tazas de leche
media taza de azúcar y unos granitos de sal.

And you need two cups of rice,
two cups of water,
some cinnamon sticks,
four cups of milk,
half a cup of sugar and a pinch of salt.

Riega el arroz en la olla.
Chiquito blanquito
el arrocito al ir cayendo
comienza a llover su música y a cantar.
En la cocina está cantando el arroz.
En la cocina está lloviendo
lluvia de gotitas blancas.

Sprinkle the rice into the pot.
The little white grains of rice
rain music and sing
as they fall.
In the kitchen the rice is singing.
In the kitchen it is raining
little white grain drops.

Ahora llena la olla con agua
hasta cubrir el arrocito.
El agua saliendo del chorro
me hace sentir que en la cocina
hay una quebrada.

Now fill the pot with water
until it covers the rice.
The water splashing from the tap
makes me feel like
there is a creek flowing through thc kitchcn.

Pon la olla en la estufa*
y comienza a cocinar el arroz
a fuego lento.
Las llamas calentando la olla
son manos de arco iris.
En la cocina hay un arco iris
abrazando la olla.

Put the pot on the stove*
and start to cook the rice
at a low temperature.
The flames heating the pot
are rainbow hands.
In the kitchen there is a rainbow
hugging the pot.

En minutitos
el agüita hierve
haciendo burbujitas
y musiquita de maracas.

In just a few minutes
the water boils,
making little bubbles
and maraca music.

Luego el agüita desaparece.
La cocina está llena de magia.
La olla está llena de espuma, olas y nubes.
En la olla hay
un cielo y también un mar.
El arrocito se ha convertido en peces
y pajaritos blancos.
Globos panzoncitos
flotan en el agua.

Soon the water disappears.
There is magic in the kitchen.
Foamy waves and clouds turn the pot
into sea and sky.
The rice has become fishies
and white birds.
Chubby little bubbles
float in the water.

Corre a la refrigeradora.
Saca la leche.
La leche al derramarse en la olla*
se vuelve una cascada.
En la cocina hay una cascada de agua blanca.

Run to the fridge
and take out the milk.
When you pour it into the pot*
the milk becomes a waterfall.
There is a white waterfall in the kitchen.

Sigue cocinando a fuego lento.*
Agrégale rajitas de canela.
Mueve el arroz despacito
haciendo remolinitos
con el cucharón de madera.
La canela flota como balsas
en el cielo mar de la olla.

Keep cooking over a low fire.*
Add the cinnamon sticks.
Slowly stir the rice,
swirling little whirlpools
with a wooden spoon.
The cinnamon sticks float like rafts
on the pot's sky sea.

No olvides la sal y el azúcar.
Toma el salero
y bailando*
agítalo hasta que salgan estrellitas.
Después te toca añadir*
más nubecitas y nieve del azucarero.

Está nevando.
Está lloviendo
en la cocina.
Están cayendo estrellitas
y nieve de tu mano.

Don't forget the salt and the sugar.
Take the salt cellar and dance around.*
Shake it until little stars come out.
Next it's time to add*
more clouds and sugar snow.

It's snowing.
It's raining
in the kitchen.
Salt stars and sugar snow
are falling from your hand.

La leche se ha secado casi por completo.
Tu mami va a decir:
—Mmmmm qué rico huele la canela.
Qué delicioso huele el arroz.
Mmmmm qué dulce huele la casa.

The milk has almost disappeared.
Your mom will say,
"Mmmmm that cinnamon smells good.
The rice smells delicious.
Mmmmm the house smells so sweet."

Ya está listo el arroz con leche.
Siéntate con toda tu familia
a comer y a beber arroz con leche.

The rice pudding is ready.
Sit down with your whole family
to slurp up the rice pudding.

El humito saliendo de los platos hondos
sube deliciosamente hacia el cielo.
Veo cadenitas de
corazones y diademas de colores.

The steam rising from the bowls
climbs deliciously to the ceiling.
I see little chains of
hearts and colored ribbons.